Laws of King George V of Georgia

Oliver Wardrop

Sir Oliver Wardrop, *Laws of King George V, of Georgia, Surnamed "The Brilliant"*, The Journal of the Royal Asiatic Society of Great Britain and Ireland, (Jul., 1914), Cambridge University Press, pp. 607-626.

ISBN: 9941957460
ISBN-13: 978-9941-9574-6-8

George V the Brilliant (1289–1346) *(Giorgi V Brtskinvale)* was the King of Georgia in the 13th and 14th centuries. He recovered Georgia from a century-long Mongol domination, restoring the country's previous strength and Christian culture. (More about the King Giorgi the Brilliant see: D. M. Lang, Georgia in the Reign of Giorgi the Brilliant (1314-1346), *Bulletin of the School of Oriental and African Studies, University of London,* Vol. 17, No. 1 (1955), pp. 74-91).

LAWS OF KING GEORGE V,
OF GEORGIA,
SURNAMED "THE BRILLIANT"

FROM THE BODLEIAN MS. OF THE CODE OF VAKHTANG VI, FORMERLY THE PROPERTY OF PRINCE DAVID OF GEORGIA

THE following translation is made from a MS. of Vakhtang's Code of Laws, purchased from a dealer in Tiflis in January, 1911, which is now the property of the Bodleian Library. The MS. is in good condition and bound in wooden boards covered with stamped leather. It is on yellow glazed paper, watermarked 1746, paged from 1 to 851; and then there follows, unpaged, a Code compiled by Prince David, son and heir of the last King of Georgia, which was hitherto unknown and bears that prince's autograph with the date "November 20, 1800" and a colophon by Gabriel, priest of Anchiskhati Church, dated 1805. The size of the page is 12 by 8 inches, of the text 8 ½ by 5 ½ inches. There are eighteen lines to the page and eight folios to the quire. A note on p. 57 says it was written by Ose Decanozishvili by the King's command in 1750, but this entry seems to have been made later in lighter ink and may only refer to the index. A remarkable feature of the MS. is that certain words (apparently those about which the scribe felt some doubt) are marked "or"; this seems to show a conscientious transcription of an old original. The MS. begins with an alphabetical list of contents (paged 1-57), the earlier part of which had apparently been lost before the pages were numbered. Then comes the usual tabular index of subjects (pp. (62-136), with references to all the sections of the code for comparative purposes, so that the laws of Vakhtang, George, the Athabegs, and the Catholicos may be compared with each other, and with Greek, Armenian, and Mosaic legislation, at a glance. On p. 142 (which bears the note showing that it was the property of Prince David, son of King George XIII) is Vakhtangs Introduction, followed by the Mosaic Law (p. 147), the Greek (Byzantine) Code of Leo VI (A.D. 886-- 912), Constantine Porphyrogenitus (A.D. 912-59), and other emperors (p. 172). Between pp. 236 (art. 147 of the Greek Code) and 448 (art. 203 of the Armenian Code of Mekhitar) 212 pages are missing. The Armenian Code ends on p. 620. On p. 624 begin the Laws of the Catholicos of Georgia; p. 639, the Laws of George V (which we hereafter translate); p. 660, the Laws of the Athabegs Aghbugha and Beka; pp. 714-851, the Code of Vakhtang and (p. 825) rules for writing judgments.

All this mass of legislation is only known in Europe by hearsay. It is of extraordinary interest to students of comparative jurisprudence; and the large section which bears the name of Vakhtang, though edited by that prince in the eighteenth century, is based upon the most ancient customs of the Georgian race and might profitably engage the attention of Assyriologists. There appeared in 1828, for the use of officials in the Caucasus, a Russian translation of the Georgian Laws, issued by the Ruling Senate; but by 1887 it had become so rare that a new edition with a preface was published in that year at Tiflis by A. S. Frenkel & D. Z. Bakradze under the title Сборникъ Законовъ грузинскаго царя Вахтанга VI. A liberal use has been made of Bakradze's notes, and the Russian translation has been an invaluable aid to the interpretation of the text. From a manuscript German version of this publication Dr. Felix Holldack prepared his book *Zwei Gmndsteine zu einer Grusinischen Staats- und Rechtsgeschichte* (Leipzig, 1907). The great Georgian scholar, M.-F. Brosset, had made a complete French translation of Vakhtang's Code and sent it to the printers, but it never saw the light. Professor Maxim Kovalevsky in his Законъ и обычаи на Кавказе (Moscow, 1890) has made use of Frenkel & Bakradze's edition. In Georgian there are a few monographs on the subject, including N. Urbneli's accounts of the Laws of George V and the Laws of the Athabegs. There is not even a published text with which to collate our MS. The only section published in Georgian up to the present time is that bearing the name of the Athabegs Aghbugha and Beka (A.D. 1361-91 and 1444-51), which was incorporated by D. Chubinov in his Chrestomathy (St. Petersburg, 1863). Mr. Sargis Cacabadze has just printed on a sheet, apparently with a view to publication in some more complete form, the Laws of King George V. He does not give any information about the source from which the text is taken, but his variants are of little importance. He dates the Laws between 1325 and 1338 A.D.

The Laws of George are the oldest original fragments of Georgian legislation. For the present it must suffice to present an English translation and a few explanatory notes. The reader should remember that these Laws are not those of the kingdom of Georgia, but ordinances, influenced by Georgian law and based on the customs of a remote and disorderly district and designed to pacify that district. Though of local application they are founded on those general Georgian principles of jurisprudence which were held in common by both highlanders and lowlanders.

Most of the MSS. of Vakhtang's Code contains only the legislation peculiarly associated with that prince's name. We have, however, in the Bodleian Library another complete text written in 1819 by Nicoloz Balinovi, but it cannot be compared in value with the much older text we have used. It may be added that Vakhtang compiled his Code before 1709 A. D. and that its adoption in Bokhara was recently proposed, and it is said to have been translated into the Sart language of that State for the purpose.

Laws of King George[1]
The Statute[2] of George, king of kings

WE, Giorgi, king of kings, son of the excellent-among-all king of kings, Dimitri, by the grace of God established this ordinance at the time when we entered into the Highlands (Mthiuli) for the survey thereof as the inalienable heritage of our realm and integral territory of our throne and scepter. We set forth from our metropolis and arrived at our palace of Zhinvani[3]; and thence we went to Khada-Tzkhaoti,[4] and we summoned all the disaffected Elders of the Glens and the Notables[5] and heard their statements and investigated their affair, and on arrival at Dariel[6] we learned that the cause wherefore the worshipful kings, crowned of God and of blessed memory, our predecessors, had not of old established a firm statute concerning the penalty for bloodshed and for divers other deeds of lawless violence was that some of them, guided by circumstances and of their good pleasure, suffered disorders among the Highlanders, while others, by reason that the times were unpropitious, failed to make ordinances for the suppression of disorders among them. But we, with God's help, on our journey back from Dariel,

---

[1] The translator has to thank Mr. M. Tscretheli for his kindness in reading through this translation in MS. and making several valuable suggestions.

[2] Dzeglis dadeba, "the setting up of the pillar, or column"; cf. Brosset, *Hist. de la Georgie*, i, pp. 648-9; Laws of Vakhtang, § 102; *Dasturlamala*, i, §§ 23, 60, and ii, §§ 1-23.

[3] In Cakhethi, at the junction of the two Aragvis, "grande et forte citadelle, ville autrefois, maintenant deserte" (Brosset, *Wakhoucht: Descr. géogr.* 299).

[4] "Résidence royale", in Mthiulethi (*Descr. géogr.*, 475, 223, 231).

[5] *Herovani.* Urbneli uses the form *haerovani.* There are some who translate as "people", deriving from *eri.*

[6] The fortress commanding the road over Mount Caucasus; "residence royale, où s'arrêtaient les souverains dans leurs expéditions contre l'Oseth" (*Descr. géogr.*, 229).

having prayed before the Grand Martyr (St. George) at Lomisa,[7] and, having gone down and settled local matters in the Tzkhra Zma[8] Glen, returned to Mukhrani[9] as our winter quarters and thence fared to the metropolis and took with us the chiefs *(eristhavni)* of the various territories *(themi)*,[10] Headmen of the Glens, Elders, and Notables. We summoned to the session the holy lord *(meuphe* = king) Catholicos of Karthli Euthymius, the Vazirs, the Bishops, and the Mouravis,[11] and found on inquiry that much disorder and violence of one upon another took place, and, because of the lightness of the penalty for bloodshed, were esteemed trivial; treacherous assaults of one upon another, pulling down of strongholds, manslaughter, carrying off wives and desertion without lawful cause, and many kinds of violence, so that no sort of justice was any longer observed. On this account, without entering into examination of past cases, for that it was impossible to grant unto each the fitting compensation , we deemed it well henceforth to ordain rules for guidance in the future as to the penalty for blood to be exacted for all and every crime, (in the region) beginning from Cross Mountain[12], in Khada Tzkhaoti, the Zanduci[13] Glen, Cibethi, Kveshethi, and

---

[7] *Descr, géogr.*, 223. This has always been the most sacred Christian shrine for the mountaineers, and their most binding oath is by St. George and Lomisa ; cf. § 42 *infra.*

[8] *Descr, géogr.*, 223, 233. A mountain and river, the latter running from Lomisa to join the River Ksan.

[9] *Descr, géogr.*, 217. "Un bel endroit et une residence royale," near the confluence of the Rivers Ksan and Mtcvari (Kura).

[10] Greek *thême*; ? clan; cf. Rambaud, *L'empire grec au xe siècle*, 175-80; Lebeau, *Hist. du Bas Empire*, xi, 401 ; *Laws of Vakhtang*, § 250.

[11] Head of a city, district, village. In this case perhaps synonym of *gamgebeli* = steward.

[12] On modern Russian maps "Крестовая гора", in Georgian "Jvaris Mta"; the summit of the pass over the Caucasus (Descr. géogr., 213).

[13] Descr. géogr., 219. On the military road near Ananur.

higher up than Menes, in judicial and ecclesiastical cases and various other matters, such as manslaughter, sacrilege, desertion of wives without lawful reasons, or their abduction. In other cases relating to religion, the investigation pertains to the Catholicos, and according to their ordinances let the bishops make inquisition. We only for civil and criminal cases have ordained the following rules to be henceforth observed.[14]

---

[14] D. Bakradze here gives a note which is summarized as follows: George V, who expelled the Mongols and for a short period welded the fragments of Georgia into a whole, and organized the civil and ecclesiastical administration, designed these Laws to reform the manners of the Georgian population at the headwaters of the Aragvi and Ksan. His Laws are monuments of the language as well as the jurisprudence of Georgia, but many of the terms need explanation. The Highlanders were under tiie local Eristhavni (Chiefs) of Ksan and Aragvi, under whom were Mouravni or Gamgebelni (Stewards), Khevis Thavni (Heads of Glens), Khevis Berni (Elders of Glens), and Mamasakhlisni (lit. house fathers). Important cases passed, with reports from the Eristhavni and Mouravni, through the Vezir (Vaziri, Chief Minister of the Crown) to the Darbazi (assembly, council, court). Vendetta was so common in the Highlands that it had to be legalized. There seems to have been, previous to these Laws, no recognition of the rights of the Crown, or of the central Church, or of landlords; order and law were eclipsed. In the Laws of George, and in those of Aghbugha and Beka, a century and more later, the professional judge does not yet appear; cases are settled by Shuani (intermediaries, mediators), or Bdcheni, whose task it was to compromise matters without recourse to judicial forms. The Bdcheui seem to have been chosen by the parties interested. Bdohe in the *Laws of Vakhtang* (§ 215) has already the sense of official arbitrator, but even then there was no organized judicial body, and the Mdivan Begs and Mdivanis of the eighteenth century were not professional lawyers, they were also notaries, etc., aud landlords, Mouravs and other officials judged in their own districts (cf. Dasturlamala). We may add that the word *eristhavi* means literally "head of the people" (cf. Джаваховъ: О государств, строй древн. Грузии); he was assisted in his administration by the *gamgebeli*, his inferior in power, who replaced him in his absence. The only MS. of the Laws of George to which

1. *Murder of Eristhavi.* - Since up to the present time no one has dared to slay an Eristhavi, so in the future let none venture to do so. But if God shall be wroth with any man and he commit so great a crime and kill an Eristhavi, according as it is so monstrous and immeasurable a misdeed, so on the judgment of the Kings Council let him be exceedingly greatly punished and mulcted: deprived of estate, expelled from his patrimony, and subjected to the penalty for blood according to rank. We do not here determine for what length of time such criminal shall be deprived of his property, for such misdeed is immeasurable and no case of the kind has yet happened. If it takes place, the king then reigning is free to act with all possible severity.

2. *Collective Murder of Steward.* - If a whole district *(kveqana)*, or one village, or an individual, or a glen slay a steward *(ganmgebeli)* while he is serving *(msakhuri)*[15] as steward, the wergild of 6,000 pieces of silver[16] is to be exacted, and, moreover, an enumeration of the men taking part in the murder having been made,[17] an impost, as of old established, once for all shall be laid on them for ever to furnish every year one horse for the service[18] of the Crown.

Bakradze had access was the copy which had belonged to Prince Theimuraz.

[15] Nob of noble birth; cf. § 4, *infra.* Or perhaps the phrase means "et an officer be steward" (?). For *msakhuri* in the sense of "veteran" cf. *Laws of Vakhtang,* § 32.

[16] *Thethri*; cf. Brosset, *Hist, de la Géorgie,* Introd., lxxxi.

[17] The text of this passage is very obscure and the translation is doubtful.

[18] *Begara* = statutory labour (French *corvée).*

3. *Murder of a Steward.* - He who chances singlehanded to slay a steward is to be punished by expulsion from his estate and confiscation thereof for ever by the Crown. If he be unable to pay in addition the wergild, the Council may hand over the slayers property to the victim's family, or leave the property to the Crown, the king himself paying for the blood.

4. *Murder of Noble Steward.* - If the steward be of noble birth and they kill him, wergild is to be exacted according to his rank.

5. *Murder of Steward by Elder of Glen.* - If the Elder of a Glen slay a steward he is to be banished for three years from his estate, his stronghold and estate are to be taken by the Crown, and the Eristhavi is to take the management of his house. After the three years, on his return, he addresses a petition to the Eristhavi, who makes a report concerning him through the Vezir[19] to the Royal Council, which restores to the Elder of the Glen his estate; but lie must give compensation for the blood of the steward according to the ordinance above set forth, and in addition he shall lose the rank of Elder of the Glen. And if anyone of the kinsfolk of that Elder of the Glen be found not to have partaken, whether patently or privily, in the murder of the steward, the Council shall appoint that man to be Elder of the Glen; and if there be no one of his blood, then the Eristhavi and the new steward shall choose some

---

[19] The *vizir, vezir, vazir,* or, in the older native form of the title, *ezoth-modzghvari,* was the Governor of the Royal Court, and in all matters the king's first counsellor. Sometimes he was an ecclesiastic of high rank *(Descr, géogr.,* 20, 40; *Hist, de la Géorgie,* 307-8). He and the other officers of the Court formed the Royal Council.

man loyal to the king and eminent in the community, and the Royal Council shall appoint him Elder of the Glen.

6. *Killing of one Elder by another.* - As regards Elders of Glens, we have thus ordained: If an Elder of a Glen slay another Elder of a Glen, he is to be banished from his patrimony for three years, the Eristhavi and the steward are to take his house in hand, the patrimony is to be seized by the Crown for three years. In the third year he petitions the Eristhavi and the steward and they report through the Vezir to the Council, and the patrimony is restored to him and he pays the wergild of 6,000 pieces of silver.

7. *Murders in families of Elders.* - If any kinsman of an Elder of a Glen slay an unpartitioned kinsman of his residing with him - father, uncle, brother, cousin, nephew, or any other of his near kin, there shall be exacted from this slayer also 6,000 silver pieces, he shall be banished from his patrimony for two years, and the Eristhavi and steward shall take his house into their hands ; and his patrimony is afterwards restored to him, according to the above ordinance (§ 6), on the report of the Eristhavi and the steward through the Vezirs and Mouravs to the Council.

8. *Collective Murder of Elder.* - And if a community (or glen-*kveqana)* slay the Elder of the Glen it is subject to the same penalty, impost of statutory labor[20] and wergild, as for the killing of a steward, and the impost shall be for ever.

9. *Murder of Elders Kinsman.* - And if a man slay a partitioned kinsman of an Elder of a Glen, whether a

---

[20] *Begara* = French *corrée.*

brother or any other near relation, he shall for such partitioned kinsman pay a wergild of 3,000 pieces of silver, and be banished for two years and his patrimony shall be seized by the Crown. After two years he shall through the Eristhavi and steward appeal in the manner above described to the Council by means of the Vezirs, and on their motion and by order of the Council his patrimony is thereupon restored to him.

10. *Near and distant Kinsmen of Elders.* - We have not ordained an equal wergild for the distant and partitioned kinsfolk and the nearest and unpartitioned kinsfolk of an Elder of a Glen. For though they be all kinsfolk dwelling under the headship of the Elder of the Glen, appointed by the Council to be the leader in war of his glen, and near to him, nevertheless as to them that are partitioned we ordain a wergild for distant kinsfolk not equal to that of near kin, but one-half thereof.

11. *Murder of Notables.* - Concerning Notables, we thus ordain: Any Notable who slays another Notable is to be banished for three years, subjected to a wergild of 200 drahcanis, or 1,200 pieces of silver,[21] and his patrimony is to be seized by the Crown. And if he be worthy of the cognizance of the Council, then, in accordance with the above ordinance, the Eristhavi and the steward having reported to the Council, shall restore to him his patrimony. But if he be not worthy of the cognizance of the Council, the Eristhavi and the steward may not let him in again and restore his patrimony.

---

[21] *The* drahcani *thus* = 6 thetris; *cf.* Brosset, Hist. de la Géorgie, *Introd., clxxviii.*

12. *Murder of Notable by Elder.* - If an Elder of a Glen slay a Notable in order to take his patrimony, let him be banished from his patrimony for a year; should the killing happen involuntarily, let him pay as Ave have above ordained.

13. *Murder of Castellan of Khada.* - In Khada there shall be two castellans. The rule is that if a resident of Khada, an Elder of a Glen or any other person, slay a Castellan appointed by authority and not divested of the command, he shall be banished from his patrimony for three years, and his patrimony shall be seized by the Crown and a wergild of 3,500 pieces of silver shall be exacted from him. After three years he may return and his patrimony shall be restored to him according to the foregoing rule and ordinance.

14. *Murder of ex-Castellan.* - If anyone shall slay a dweller in Khada who is not Castellan, but has been formerly appointed Castellan and is no longer Castellan, he shall pay wergild as for a Notable, and shall be banished from his patrimony for the period we have ordained above for a Notable; he shall afterwards return after the form above prescribed. And if anyone slays a Castellans brother or son he shall pay wergild as for a Notable.

15. *Parricide.* - It is unnatural for children to slay their parents, and God avert such audacity! And if God be wroth with any man and he attempt this, he deserves whatever is worst, every misfortune and misery, capital punishment, eternal banishment, uprooting, and destruction. For such a crime we ordain no wergild; it would be monstrous, unseemly, and unnatural, and become an example for others. Nor is it natural to subject strangers sharing with children in the murder of parents to

the same penalty with them, and for this we fix no wergild because in our times it has not happened, and God grant that it may not.

16. *Tenure by Service.* - If a father grows old and his son has grown up and the father be not able to serve the king (*batoni*), it is more fitting for them to dwell together, and if for any reason they cannot do this and the purchased estate (i.e. the property the father has acquired in addition to his patrimony) be adequate, let the father take the purchased property and let the son do service to us with the patrimony, and if the purchased property be inadequate for the father, let there be an allotment made also from the patrimony. And if (the father) agree with the son the purchased estate also passes to the son, but if he agree not the son has no power over the purchased estate. If the father wishes he may sell it and if he wishes he may bring in the buyer (into possession).[22] The father may do what seems good to him; the son cannot claim the purchased property.

17. *Fratricide.* - If God be wroth with anyone and brother slays brother, let that murderer be banished for ten years from his patrimony and let the estate be seized by the Crown. And in the tenth year let him petition the Eristhavi and the steward. They shall report to the Vezirs, the Vezirs lay the matter before the Council, and the man is permitted to return. According to the rank so shall he pay wergild and shall again be granted the patrimony, and if there be not surviving a son of that slain man, nor any unpartitioned kinsman, that brother as wergild for his brother shall be mulcted of one half of the patrimony for

---

[22] The text is obscure.

his brothers soul's sake[23] and half shall be seized by the Crown. And that half wergild ordained for the soul's sake shall be handed over to any surviving kinsman of the slain man who shall provide for his soul, and if there be none such survivor the Eristhavi and the steward shall give it into the hands of the clergy and laity[24] of that community.

18. *Disposal of Victim's Estate*, - And if there be four, five brothers, however much they may be partitioned, the nearest of kin shall take and use it for his soul, and if that slain man have left a wife and she do not remarry, from the wergild of that slain man there shall be allotted to her, so far as possible, an alimony; and if they be worthy of the cognizance of the Council let the Council be appealed to and let. it be ordained by the Council, and if they be not worthy let the Eristhavi and the steward ordain and assign to her from the wergild one-tenth part.

19. *Tenure by Service*. - Touching campaigns, Ave thus ordain: Whatever glen *(kveqana)* or community *(themi)* the Eristhavi and the steward summon by (royal) command and they do not come forth in due time, that glen or village, or be it one man, however many men be lacking to the host they shall not be pardoned for one year and their patrimony shall be seized for the Crown and one ox per homestead shall be driven off for the Crown ; and in the second year the patrimony shall be restored through the good offices of the Eristhavi and the steward. This applies both to Notables and villagers, and if an Elder of a Glen be lacking and go not forth, his Eldership of the Glen and his patrimony shall be taken away ; and after one

---

[23] Vakhtang's Code, §§ 224, 248.
[24] Our MS. reads "men"; Cacabadze reads "Catholicos".

year his patrimony shall be regranted, if he be meritorious and have committed no other crime.

20. *Substituted Service.* - If an Elder of a Glen be unwell at the time of a campaign his brother and nearest kinsman must go forth, and the Elder of the Glen shall be forgiven for not going to the host.

21. *Wife Desertion.* - If a man desert his wife without cause and she be faultless towards him, and he separate from her, he shall pay half the wergild due to that woman's rank.[25]

22. *Wife-stealing.* - If a man ravish another man's wife, however much her husband may have burned, carried off, looted of the ravisher's property during a year, even if the value thereof exceed the compensation due for such a deed, is not to be set down in the account; but after one year, whatever hostilities lie commits are to be counted and the ravisher is only bound to pay him half the wergild according to rank. If during the hostilities he slays any one of the ravishers' men, this murder is reckoned to his account in computing the wergild, excepting the ravisher himself, concerning whom we have ordained hereafter.

23. *Abduction without adultery.* - If a man carries off a wedded[26] wife, if they have not had carnal connection, he shall pay half the wergild according to rank.

---

[25] Cf. § 25, *infra.*
[26] Lit. "crown-blest".

24. Abduction of Betrothed. - If a man carries off a betrothed bride[27] he shall pay one-sixth of the wergild according to rank.

25. Wife Desertion. - He who deserts his wife without cause, and it shall appear that though she was not at fault in anything yet he has separated from her innocent, shall pay half the wergild according to her rank.[28]

26. *Reprisals for Wife-stealing.* - If a man carry off a man's wife, it is ordained above how the ravisher may be treated as an enemy,[29] and if the husband make an attack when they are not yet reconciled, have not yet affiance one in the other, and wergild has not yet been paid, the husband shall not be considered an aggressor even if he slay. When they both meet and fight and the ravisher is slain, the Catholicos and the Bishops fix a fine for the requiem; and if the woman take part in the fight and be armed and be slain, no wergild is to be paid for that woman, but if the slain woman be innocent[30] double wergild shall be paid for her, and for a wound[31] it is equal for all: monks, priests, and women who are nuns;[32] and if the woman be not a nun double wergild shall not be paid and the wergild shall be equal; for monks, deacons, priests, and women the wergild is double. And if any such be without cause slain or wounded, compensation shall be paid according to

---

[27] Lit. "cross-exchanges wife"; cf. *Laws of Aghbugha*, § 40.

[28] Cf. *supra*, § 21.

[29] § 22.

[30] Bakradze says some interpret "a stranger, outsider".

[31] *Gershi*; cf. Professor Marr's monograph on the word *gershi*, also the Georgian version of Leviticum xxiv, 19, 20 and §§ 29, 32, *infra*.

[32] *Mtsirveli* = servant of God; cv. Chubinov's Dictionary.

their rank. If a monk or a secular priest or a woman come as mediator, if it so be that they are not armed and be thus slain, whoever slays them shall pay double wergild according to their rank.

27. Burg-bryce: Private War. - If anyone without the command of the Council destroy another's stronghold, whether he be an Elder of a Glen, or a community against a community, or an equal against an equal, in a word, whoever he may be, and the destruction takes place by reason of enmity and there be between them any suit at law, such suit shall be decided in accordance with our ordinance; and for the destruction of the stronghold half wergild according to rank shall be exacted, and according to the rank of the lord of the castle the destroyer shall rebuild the castle suitably. And if there be an order (of the Council) and they destroy by command they have no responsibility and nothing is due from them.

28. Escheats: Tenure by Service. - If any untilled patrimony be left an escheat because the owner has disappeared, and men of his family be discovered, it is to be granted to them that are nearest to him in kin and in the sharing of sorrow and joy, so that the community lack not the commissariat, military service, and statutory labor. And should none of their family be left and some other man worthy of a grant from the Council assume the burdens of commissariat, statutory labor, and military service, let the Council make the grant to him. And if he be one who is unworthy of a grant from the Council, let the Eristhavi and the steward hand it over to him so that he perform the statutory labor and service.[33]

29. *Resistance to Authority.* - Concerning aggressors we ordain: He who having a dispute with another asks for judgment and the defendant goes not to plead, then applies to the steward and says, "I have asked this man to plead and he has not appeared." The steward shall report this to the Eristhavi,[34] and the man shall be summoned twice, thrice to judgment. If he appear not either on the summons of the Eristhavi or on that of the steward, and trustworthy, unprejudiced, and disinterested witnesses declare that he had been summoned to justice three times but appeared not, should the plaintiff make an attack upon the defendant, however many may be killed and wounded on either side, the wergild and smart- money are to be equal on both sides, for the aggressor and the resident, inasmuch as the latter was called three times and appeared not. The Eristhavi and the steward testify that their man came and the defendant presented himself not for judgment, therefore the aggressor and his victim have their wergild equalized after their rank, according to the families of the men. When the raid is made upon a man who was employed on the errands of the Council and thus

---

[33] Bakradze. In Karthli, Caklietlii, and Imerethi escheats became the property of the Crown, the landlord, or the Church, according to the overlordship in each case; but they were almost always regranted, either to distant kinsfolk or, failing them, other men of merit; cf. *Laws of Vakhtang,* §§ 232, 248; *Customs,* § 31; Brosset, *Hist, de la Georgie,* ii, livr. ii, p. 480. Among the mountaineers there seems to have been no rule prior to this enactment.

[34] The text is not clear. An alternative reading is : "He who having a dispute with another summons him two or three times to justice, and the party summoned goes not, must, appearing before the steward, explain the matter to him, and he is bound to report to the Eristhavi."

received not the first and last summons of the Eristhavi
and steward, and was thus raided without just cause, then
the aggressor has no wergild; however many may be slain
it is naught, and to that man and that community who
have been raided it is just that for all, so many as are
innocent, whom the raider shall slay, for all he shall pay
according to their rank.

30. *Reprisals for Wife-stealing and Murder: Prices for
Outrage.* - If any man steal another's wife or slay any
guiltless person, and the man make a raid upon that
murderer and wife-stealer because of the outrage, he is not
called an aggressor.[35] Of patrimony or anything else, thus
it is: To him whose wergild is 12,000 pieces of silver, for hi
in the price of one injury is 300 pieces of silver, for
noblemen (who are) Elders of Glens 150 pieces of silver
for one injury.

31. *Outrages on Notables.* - For Notables a compensation
of thirty pieces of silver, and we have thus ordained: To all
whether great or small according to the amount of the
wergild.

32. *Disfiguring Wounds.* - Let it be thus with regard to
smart-money: He on whose face an indelible wound shall
be inflicted, or whose nose shall be cut off, shall receive
one-fifth of the wergild of his rank. If the wound be on a
visible part but without mutilation thereof, the penalty

---

[35] The remainder of this paragraph should form a separate section, and
thus the reduplication above in §§ 21 and 25 would bo avoided while
preserving the number of articles in the statute.

shall be that for three injuries and the price of the medicine of the surgeons.

33. *Loss of Right Hand.* - In the matter of members of the body, we thus ordain: To him whose right hand is cut off or mutilated by wounding, one-third of the wergild is due.

34. *Left-handed Men.* - If a man be left-handed and use his left hand as a right hand, he receives for the cutting off of the left hand as if it were the right hand.

35. *Loss of Eye or Foot.* - If a man s eye is put out or his foot mutilated or cutoff, the fourth part of the wergild is levied.

36. *Hands, Feet, Eyes.* - For mutilation in an affray of both hands, or feet, or eyes, half wergild is due, according to his rank, and the price of the medicine of the surgeons, whatever be expended; for mutilation of any one of these in an affray, but not of two together, it shall be as we have above ordained.

37. *Thumb and Fingers.* - If a man cut off or mutilates another's thumb, half the compensation appointed for the hand is to be levied, according as it be the right or left hand, and for cutting off or maiming any other finger, one-third of the compensation for the hand is to be levied.

38. *Hidden Wounds.* - Wherever a man be wounded so that by reason of the clothing it is not seen, nor is there any mutilation on account of the wounding, each shall be compensated by the price of one injury, according to rank, and he shall also be paid the price of the medicine of the surgeon, whatever has been spent.

39. *Front Teeth.* - If a man knocks out any of a man's four upper front teeth or four lower front teeth, for each tooth of those which are visible he shall pay the price for two injuries according to condition and rank.

40. *Other Teeth.* - For knocking out the other invisible teeth beyond those four, for each tooth he shall pay the price of one injury.

41. *Killing or Wounding of "Comrades".* - Should anyone take to himself a comrade[36] and he is slain or wounded, no wergild is due from the slayer nor shall smart-money be paid. And with regard to him whose comrade the slain or wounded man was, let it be as follows: If there were between them a pact that they should be comrades one to the other and live and die together, then they are subject to equal responsibility for everything. And if they should for any reason separate and there be none of the kinsfolk of the slain man to pay wergild, then he is bound to pay for the blood of his comrade, out of the booty received, a compensation suitable to rank and to compensate in full

---

[36] Asabia. The reference is probably to sworn brothers who had made a pact of adelphopoiia ; cf. note to p. 48 of Rusthavcli's Man in the Panther's Skin (vol. xxi, Oriental Translation Fund, New Series). It is evident that the association was for the purpose of brigandage. M. Tseretheli says: "I think *asabia* is an Arabic borrowed word. *sahaba* = to be a comrade."

him who has been robbed, and if there be no booty he has nothing to pay.[37]

42. *Killing of Peasants of Lomisa.* - He who slays a peasant of Lomisa[38] who has been presented thereto by the king or by anyone else shall be fined 1,500 pieces of silver. From of old the boundaries of Lomisa have been ordained: the hither side of Khada to Tzkhaoti, and so let it be ordained.

43. *Confederacies forbidden.* - Elders of Glens and Notables dwelling on this side must not unite themselves with those dwelling on the farther side in any military expeditions or civil matters saving those affecting their own Eristhavi's district, on pain of deprivation by the Council of estate and destruction of stronghold.

44. *Horse- and Cattle-stealing.* - Concerning brigandage we thus ordain: If any man steal a horse, sheep, cow, or other beast, or forcibly break into a house and carry off anything, and thereafter fight with the pursuers who have overtaken him and be slain, however many such brigands be slain no penalty is to be exacted for their blood; but, on the other hand, there shall be handed over to them that have been robbed, in satisfaction for the robbery, the

---

[37] The text of the second half of this paragraph is almost unintelligible.

[38] This church, dedicated to St. George, is situated on one of the tributaries of the River Ksan, on the ridge of Lomisis Mtlia, on the boundaries of the districts of Mthiulethi, Zhanuri, and Tzkhra Znm (Descr. géogr., 223).

leader himself and two others of his band. Should the robbers slay the owner or anyone on his side during the pursuit, full wergild is to be exacted for all the slain and thrice the value of what was stolen.

45. *Reprisals for Theft when justice is delayed.* - If anything be stolen from a man by anybody and the thief cannot be discovered at that time, but they afterwards find the stolen property and the truth be revealed and the man go and ask for redress, whether the community or an individual have been the robber, when the owner of the property goes and petitions he has right on his side and they must make restitution and proper compensation according to the preceding ordinance. And if they do not so, he shall inform the steward and he shall tell the Elder of the Glen of that community and they shall exact the penalty fixed by that ordinance; and if they heed not his summons and he petition twice, thrice, if there be an Eristhavi in the neighborhood let him be informed, and if he exact not the compensation and the owner of the property make a raid upon that brigand, he is not to be considered an aggressor, nor is he to be called upon for wergild for the thief or any of his comrades and associates whom he may slay in fight, but however many may be slain on the side of the owner of the property, for all of them wergild shall be exacted because the brigands have refused (to restore his property)[39] and the steward and the Elders of the Glen testify that the brigands were summoned twice, thrice, and so their wergild is naught.

46. *Money Pleas, Usury.* - Concerning debt we have thus ordained: The taking of interest is not in accordance with

---

[39] Translation doubtful.

the Georgian laws, nor is it prescribed by other laws, and interest is unnatural. But if for any reason a lender be so wicked that he levies interest, whatsoever time shall have elapsed let him have two pieces of silver on ten.[40] However long the time that has passed let him have no more than this, nor is it just to take more, and unless he be a very wicked man it is not right that he should levy even this. Let justice thus be done of all.

---

[40] *The Laws of Aghbugha and Beka* (§ 95) also fix 20 per cent as the maximum and forbid compounf interest. *Vakhtang's Laws* (§ 125) make 12 per cent the legal rate.